WHO CARES?!

The Journey of a Caregiver...

Meagan M. Thomas

WHO CARES?! THE JOURNEY OF A CAREGIVER

By: Meagan M. Thomas

Copyright © 2014

Published by Imperial Publishers, Inc.

North Charleston, South Carolina, 29405

Scriptures noted NKJV. are taken from the NEW KING JAMES VERSION. Copyright © 1979, 1980, 1982, Thomas Nelson, Inc., Publishers.

Printed in the United States of America

ISBN-13: 978-0692223154

ISBN-10: 0692223150

CONTENTS

PREFACE

For several years I often pondered the topic of my first publication. Fortunately for me, God planted an illustration that I couldn't resist. He took me through a difficult process along the way, but every countless moment along this journey has transpired into a blessing that I only hope transforms the lives of any and everyone who reads this.

Thanks to you Mom for all the amazing things you've done thus far. Although I will never be able to repay you for all you've both done and sacrificed, thank you for allowing me the opportunity to show my love and appreciation for you every single day. I love you!

To my family, I thank you for your love, support and encouragement. It is truly your gentle hand that has helped guide me every step along the way.

To my heavenly angel, I strive harder each day to only emulate the wonderful things that you've conquered, the lives you've touched and the positivity that you always exemplified.

And to the person reading this, may I say with my sincerest gratitude, Thank You!

I only hope that this book inspires you as much as it inspired me writing it.

May these devotionals uplift you, the tips enlighten you, and all its components nourish your soul...

Meagan

INTRODUCTION

FOR ANYONE WHO'S EVER CARED FOR A LOVED ONE.

THE STRESS THAT HAS ACCUMULATED OVER TIME IS AN UNDERSTATEMENT

SLEEPLESS NIGHTS, RESCHEDULED APPOINTMENTS, COOKING, CLEANING AND MEDICINE DUTY.

LET'S REWIND TO THE BEGINNING OF IT ALL.

LET'S REWIND TO THE DAY, THE TIME, THE HOUR, THE MOMENT YOUR LIFE CHANGED

YOU COULD'VE BEEN ANYWHERE IN THE WORLD

IN FACT, YOU COULD'VE LOST YOUR LOVED ONE, BUT BY THE GRACE OF GOD YOU DIDN'T

SO HE PLACED YOU ON DUTY PATROL.

TO RESPOND TO THE NEEDS OF ONE OF HIS MOST PRIZED POSSESSIONS.

NOW LET'S FAST FORWARD TO THE VERY MOMENT THINGS FINALLY SINK IN.

NOW IT'S TIME TO GET INFORMED, ASK QUESTIONS, MAKE LEGAL DECISIONS, COOK, CLEAN, MANAGE FINANCES, AND

YES —PILE ON ANOTHER LOAD

YOU'VE REACHED THE BOILING POINT, AND QUITE FRANKLY WHO CARES?! WELL, I'LL BE ONE OF THE VERY FIRST TO SAY. I DO!!!!

I AM JUST LIKE YOU!

I AM A CAREGIVER

HERE'S TO OUR JOURNEY...

7

WHO CARES (THE JOURNEY OF A CAREGIVER?)

DID YOU KNOW?

∞

- Millions of Americans become Caregivers for family members or friends dealing with Illnesses every day.

- According to the National Alliance for Caregiving this past year, there were an estimated total of 65.7 million Americans who served as caregivers for aging and ill relatives.

- Based on the nationwide total of 'givers' every single day, approximately 1.4 of those Americans are children and teens between the ages of 8 and 18. (American psychological association).

- Sadly, caregivers are at a higher risk for emotional, mental and physical health problems that arise from complex care-giving situations.

What Is Caregiving?

When I first googled the term caregiver, several interpretations appeared. Among the many, definitions Including: a family member or paid helper, a person who helps clients with tasks, a person who provides food, clothing and shelter to someone in need; there is no single definition that clearly emphasizes the many roles a caregiver actually has.

In this book, I will illustrate both the highs and lows that come along with caregiving through my own perspective. I will also give a helpful insight as to what one can typically expect along this journey, how to prepare, what's insightful, as well as a few helpful tips to help guide you along the way.

☐ What to expect?

☐ How to adjust and cope with change?

☐ The experiencing of changes in mood (bitterness, depression, and self pity.)

☐ How to not get lost in caregiving?

☐ How to be honest with yourself, and control your attitude?

> ➢ Book will include an Informational tool kit that gives a clear and concise Interpretation of the term "caregiver."

☐ Daily Devotionals

☐ Personal Stories/testimonials

☐ Health Tips

☐ Nutritional Facts

☐ Reflection Section

New Journey

∞

"The greatest lessons you will learn will come from the toughest seasons in your life."

Today you will embark on a journey that will possibly change your entire life. Chances are your life will never go back to its normal routine, however that has absolutely no influence on the levels that God is about to take you..

They often say, in life things will tend to get worse before they become better. You will reach your lowest of lows, and be completely removed from what you personally consider to be "the comfort zone."

I remember the day my mother had her stroke as if it were yesterday. It was a typical day for me. I'd gotten off work early and opted to do a little grocery shopping for a dinner for the two of us. Lasagna and garlic bread was the main course.

I had several conversations with my mother throughout that day, and each conversation reiterated an unshakable headache that she couldn't get rid of (strike 1). The idea of my mother's headache being severe truly didn't cross my mind, since we were use to experiencing terrible sinus headaches due to unpredictable and unflattering weather.

My mother was very quiet that day. Throughout dinner there wasn't much conversation (something we're not use to). After dinner, I remember cleaning the kitchen when my mother came in and went into the cabinet for medicine. Immediately as she attempted to open the medicine bottle there came an uncontrollable stumble (strike 2).

I told my mother to go and sit, and that I'd bring her the medicine and water. Unfortunately what happened next was unimaginable. Literally within a couple of minutes of taking the medicine my mother became nauseous (strike 3). And every attempt that I made to get her up and cleaned was another vomit attack. She couldn't stop vomiting, I couldn't understand anything she was saying (strike 4), and she was uncontrollably restless (strike 5).

I remember the entire time talking to her "mom how are you feeling?" "You're scaring me!" "Are you Ok?" but I knew she wasn't. There was something seriously wrong,

Now, the next few minutes within that time period occurred so quickly that it's hard to believe they actually took place. On one phone I had my grandparents (who were 3 1/2 hours away from us) praying.

On another phone was my Aunt, and the next was a co-worker and close friend of my mother. By the time I'd called 911 my mother was in and out of consciousness. I was terrified. Neighbors wanted to know what was going on, paramedics wanted to know my mother's medical history and family and friends were in utter shock.

Riding in the ambulance was one of the scariest trips of my life. Was she ok? How long will they keep her? Will we be able to return home? No one knew.

By the time we made it to the hospital, doctors immediately rushed in to run tests on my mother. Unfortunately, my mother's pressure had escalated to 264/126. Scary!

In my opinion one of the most uninviting yet well respected places on earth is a hospital. They're cold, gloomy and often times the bearer of bad news.

That night I didn't sleep. There I sat in a small cushionless chair next to my mother's bed, with the sounds of empty echoed halls and everlasting beeps. That night became the foundation to the incomparable Journey that would change my entire life.

Point to ponder: God has a divine plan for us all, but we have to be willing to let him mold us. Will you allow him to mold you?

A Major Setup

∞

Things have yet to set in. Everything up until now quite frankly seems surreal. Lord, why now? What Next? How should I? The feeling of guilt, hurt, and confusion are typically normal at this moment. And although being strong as we face difficult situations often becomes difficult to manage, there is always encouragement to guide us through the day.

"But those who hope in the Lord

Will renew their strength.

They will soar on wings like eagles;

They will run and not grow weary,

They will walk and not be faint."

ISAIAH 40:31 (NIV)

Point to ponder: Got questions? Or are you simply questioning what God is doing in your life? Instead of saying "Why God Why?" just say "God --- I trust you."

DAY 3

Get legally prepared!

∞

"In life changing situations, not only is preparation key, but the notion of acting fast can help both you and your loved one later down the road."

Follow the checklist below for details on where to begin:

- Check the status of insurance, job status and benefits
- Based on the survivor's age and working condition, the very first step is to take initiative and inform their employer. (IF APPLICABLE)
- Gather all the patients personal information (birth certificate, social security card, driver's license)
- Always keep the original copy (make several additional duplicate copies and store the original copy in a safe place.)
- Get organized
- Get a safe, file cabinet or file organizer to stay ahead.
- Be sure to keep insurance information, social security numbers, date of birth, power of attorney and other healthcare related information handy.
- Learn all about your family member's condition.
- Find out what your family member's insurance covers. What does and doesn't it cover?
- Review or create legal documents.
- Research and assign a durable power of attorney.
- Consult with other family members/friends.
- Find out what's available in your community for your loved one.
- Think about managing the job of caregiving.

Typically when a loved one has a health or disabling condition, it immediately becomes stressful. What makes the situation even more stressful is the planning for what's ahead, both legally and financially.

Among the many decisions one will have to make during this process, there's more to think about

Including:

Long-term care, (nursing home or patient care facility) medical expenses, preparation of long-term

Health care private insurance, Medicare, Medicaid and supplemental security income (SSI)

Bills, managing family assets: ensuring that the patient's spouse and any disabled family members are adequately protected cost of living, the distribution of your loved ones personal assets upon their death. (typically their will.)

Fortunately there are resources to help guide you along the way.

First, one of the most resourceful things to do when your loved one becomes ill, or is unable to care for themselves is find an attorney who not only has knowledge of your loved ones condition but also knows the proper steps to take.

***I know what you're thinking, attorneys are expensive, and how do I go about finding an attorney who can help me? But there are options for everyone, and I do mean everyone.

Feel comfortable asking family, friends and associates on possible recommendations of attorneys who may be able to assist. If that isn't an option, another way to locate an attorney is through an attorney referral service. There are legal associations for lawyers that are found in most communities.

❖ Medical visits can become very expensive, (in my experience alone, we collected more than $30,000 dollars in hospital bills when my mother became hospitalized). It's imperative during this stage that you research and fully understand that there is help as well as government assistance available. Medicare, SSI, and Home Health Care are just a few services, not to mention the other numerous options offered for patients and Military veterans...

➢ Each state has different rules and regulations for applying for assistance, so be sure to first check with

Your state program, and follow the links below.

- For both Medicaid and Medicare

www.medicare.gov

- For power of attorney

www.legalforms.com

- Ask you local hospital's social working dept. for an advance medical power of attorney or follow

http://www.caringinfo.com.org/stateaddownload

- For social security

www.ssa.gov/pgm/disability.htm

- For government benefits

www.benefits.gov

- To apply for TennCare Choices Program (for elderly 65 and older or disabled 21 and older)
- www.tn.gov

Where to start?

"The starting point of all achievement is desire."

~Napoleon Hill

∞

The feeling may not come often but when it does it's amazing. The feeling is inevitable. It's a will to strive for greater. Desire is its name! What is it that you desire most in life right now? Is it to maintain the well being of a loved one? A new job? More rest? Social independence? A getaway? What about the life you left behind, that is before caretaking. Truth is many will avoid the responsibility of caring for a loved one primarily because the stress, buildup and responsibilities that coincide.

When my mother became ill, I often wondered what to do. What if I do something wrong? How do I know what questions to ask? Or better yet, what if something goes terribly wrong in my care?

This journey is full of illogical theories, but so is life. And in life, our experiences along the journey are the key tools we need in order for to manifest into something greater.

If God provided you with all the answers to every question, concern and occurrence in your life, will you be willing to accept the answers or shy away from what bears in front of you?

Point to ponder: Begin to take ownership and acknowledge the following steps in order to stay afloat of the obstacles that may try to defeat you.

1. Don't doubt yourself

2. Take your time

3. Breathe

4. Write things down

5. Be honest (ask questions and tell others when you're unsure.)

6. Understand that it's ok to make mistakes. (You'll learn from them.)

Things are shifting

"The same God that holds the stars in place will hold your life in place."

~Unknown

∞

It's remarkably amazing how our mood shifts based on our feelings. Have you ever heard the expression "Never make permanent decisions based on temporary feelings?" Have you ever felt as if you've reached the lowest of all lows? You're boiling point? The highest peak of your journey? With so many adjustments being set into place the shifting of your own life as well as your loved one may leave you doubtful. Fortunately, there is light in the midst of the darkness. Shift those thoughts of doubt, bitterness, and worry into thoughts of peace, free will and courage. God wants to turn those rain clouds into brighter days. Will you?

Today I declare these words:

Lord. show me how to give up the control that I've placed over my own life, and allow me the ability to accept the changes, the trials and the tribulations so that I may receive your blessings with humility. I believe it and I receive it.

Believe in yourself

"Be gentle with yourself, you're doing the best you can."

~Vicki Reece

∞

Feeling doubtful? Discouraged? Weighed down? You may ask yourself is the load too heavy, but the answer is no! Don't lose hope for yourself. Difficulties today are the ultimate setup for the joy God has set aside for you tomorrow. Unfortunately, in order to receive your voucher for joy you have to put in your request today. Believe it, and achieve it!

DAY 7

Let's be honest

∞

Ever felt like screaming? Throwing in the towel? Or maybe just being alone? Although giving up may seem easier than the load that comes along with your patience and hard work, don't allow your perception of what may appear easier to stop you in your tracks.

Let's be honest, the road ahead may not always be pleasant. In fact sometimes you'll experience inclement weather. Some days it may rain, and the next it may pour. You may experience lighting or thunderstorms, and suddenly in the midst of those rain clouds, a ray of sunshine will appear.

God is working even when you can't see it. He's already aligning your path.

Today's prayer,

Lord, keep me aligned along the path that you hath set upon me even when times are difficult. And help me to see that the good work that I do will have a harvest of righteousness.

Point to ponder: Understand that God knows that the load you're carrying is heavy, but he inevitably loves you way too much to leave you feeling discomforted.

DAY 8

Allow others in

"Sometimes what you're most afraid of doing is the very thing that will set you free."

~Robert Tew

∞

For you, everyday may be a new challenge. Some days may be better and some days you may succom the worse.

Sometimes in caretaking the feeling of expressing everything to everyone may not be a comfortable one. The point of allowing others in is simply that, **ALLOW THEM IN**. Explain your day, your tasks, challenges or a new discovery you came across. The willingness to allow others in on your insecurities, feelings, confusion and disappointments will loosen the weight from your shoulders.

Point to ponder: What do you do with your worries, concerns, and fears? Do you express them to others? Do you hold them in? Or do you give God complete ownership over them?

Read Proverbs 16:3

DAY 9

Don't leave yourself behind

"Think good thoughts. Don't worry about what's going wrong, focus on all that's going right."

~Unknown

So you can't go to the opening premiere of that new movie that you here has 5 stars. Or maybe you can't make plans to spend time with friends. Missing out? Make plans for yourself now.

Having a good time doesn't mean that you have to be in a large crowd, or away from your own environment. The true fun starts within you. Find that inner peace and enjoy your own company.

Tonight pick a nice movie, choose a new book, play your favorite relaxation music, and gather your favorite dish for a nice night in. If you're feeling alone, invite a few close friends or family members and you've got a celebration of you on your hands.

DAY 10

Don't lose yourself

"Don't lose your identity in your circumstance. You are who God says you are."

~Paula White

∞

From dusk till dawn, morning, noon, and night you unselfishly take on the title of chef, housekeeper, taxi driver, critique, judge, and personal medical assistant. But in the midst of all of those titles and the large responsibilities that come along with them, don't forget that you're only human. As amazingly as you handle every single one of the following tasks; don't forget that you're only one person.

It's so easy to become so wrapped up in our duties for our loved ones that we forget the duty that we owe to ourselves. Don't forget who you are, all the things you loved before your journey, and most importantly don't forget to take time to care for yourself.

Point to ponder- There are several chapters in your life, don't get lost in the one you're in..

Guilt-free

"When we're able to unleash the burdens that have traveled along with us over time, that is when we are truly free- free of guilt, free of sorrow, and free from what others may think."

~Meagan M. Thomas

Have you ever had that moment of complete freedom? The feeling you tend to get when you've given yourself a cheat day from your diet, bought a new handbag or outfit, even a day of indulging in your favorite activity. How was that feeling? How long has it been since you've experienced it?

Today is your guilt free day. Steal your time to do something that makes you feel free. Why not, you spend too many days during the week feeling guilty.

Don't look back

"On the true journey of life it is not what we leave behind, but what we pick up along the way to our destination."

~Unknown

∞

What is it that you've learned from caretaking? Is it more than you knew when your journey began? Chances are your answer will be yes, because it's all a part of God's will.

In order to be properly aligned with God, we must surpass the roadblocks, stubbles and turmoil. It is during this process that we both learn and receive our wisdom from God. That wisdom only helps us move a step closer into our divine purpose.

Today, stop looking back at what use to be, and seek towards what can be.

Point to ponder: As a new day approaches, so does the opportunity to become more Christ like.

Read James 1:4

Count your blessings

"Worthy is he who remembers to thank God for all his blessings, but admirable is he who still thanks God in spite of the pain."

~Unknown

Do your problems outweigh your blessings? If so, then it's time to shift your vision.

Out of the 42 billion people on this planet, there's absolutely no one who doesn't have at least one single thing to be thankful for. Trials and tribulations do not pick and choose. They impact us all. Some almost tear us apart, but they never leave us stranded.

I encourage you to count all of your blessings today and be a blessing.

Today, look for ways to use your blessing. **REMEMBER**, no blessing is ever too small.

LIVE.FOR.NOW

∞

Are you living for the moment? Are you preparing for your future? What is it that you strive for every single day? I've discovered that I learn the most about myself in the most difficult situations. Once there, I discover my fears; my insecurities, what I may consider a reasonable outcome and what can possibly stop me from moving forward in life.

What is it that has your focus at this moment? Is it a problem? An outcome? Or is your attention focused on a new opportunity?

Whatever it is, look for ways to live in the moment and make the best of it. Life is too short to live for your past and the desires of what your future may hold. Be present in your understanding and live life to the fullest.

L.O.V.E

"Love begins by taking care of the closest ones--- the ones at home."

~Mother Teresa

∞

When you think of the word love what is the first thing that comes to mind? Is it a loved one? Partner/spouse, object of affection, etc.? What about yourself? With so many obstacles, influences and distractions, we caretakers tend to forget about ourselves. We work hard, fight battles and take on a weight of the world, all while caring for a loved one. Unfortunately for us, we seldom think about loving ourselves.

Loving one another is an understatement. It often takes time, hard work and persistence, but that doesn't make it impossible. Reach past the impossible and opt for positive ways of showing your love and affection.

Point to ponder: The love of God will sustain you when nothing else will.

Read 1 Corinthians 13:2

<u>*Encourage others as well as yourself*</u>

"Keep your head up, God always gives his toughest battles to his

Strongest soldiers!"

~Evelyn M

My greatest life lessons were actually inherited from the basketful of experiences that I've learned from family, friends, and acquaintances.

Can you imagine someone who's always hot tempered, deceitful, bitter and uncontrollable of their own life giving you advice on yours? So how can you be of any encouragement to your loved one if you're feeling discouraged yourself? It doesn't take much to be uplifted, just a will to be happy and control of your joy.

This period may be one of the most difficult times you've ever experienced, but remember, storms always come to pass.

Feeling stressed or overwhelmed?

"Stress makes you believe that everything has to happen right now. Faith reassures you that everything will happen in God's timing."

~Unknown

Experiencing loss of sleep, change in appetite, discouragement and frequent mood swings? How will you pay that bill that's right around the corner? Are the frustrations of what surrounds you too much? Have you reached your limit with problems?

When I began caregiving, No one had any idea of what I was dealing with on the inside. Unfortunately, that was the worst mistake because I vented to the only person who I knew would listen, **My Mother**. Eventually that venting turned into complaining and the complaining went against everything that I knew God wanted me to do.

If I were to tell you that you wouldn't experience those rough days during your caregiving journey, I wouldn't be honest. Truth is, those days will come but the even greater thing is they also go, which ultimately allows us to grow.

So how do you get from where you are now? First, I need you to whisper these words to yourself- _"I will not fear the greatness hiding behind my storm; I will receive It."_ repeat these words until you believe in them. Don't just say them, believe in them the same way God believes in you.

As you meditate on the phrase I ask that you read the following scripture and reflect. May it give you peaceful healing.

"My brethren, count it all joy when ye fall into divers temptations.

Knowing this; that the trying of your faith worketh patience.

But let patience have her perfect work, that ye may be perfect and entire, wanting nothing."

James 1:2-3 (KJV)

Ponder on this scripture and understand that God's trials are only small tests of our faith. Will you trust God with what you're going through? Will you put your faith in him, or allow fear to steal your faith? Talk to him, confess your heart, those frustrations and be as informal as possible. He's watching, waiting to supply you with all the strength you need to pass the tests of time. Just think of the reward that God has in store for you on the other side of the storm.

Blessings!!!

When the going gets rough?

"In rough moments, remember, tomorrow is always a new opportunity to grow from the tests of life."

~Heather Lindsey

∞

Wake up on the wrong side of the bed this morning? Did you go to bed feeling uneasy, and wake up only to feel that same discomfort? Are you feeling mentally and physically exhausted?

Take a moment and Meditate on this simple prayer today.

"Lord, today I declare your favor. Shift my thoughts of unhappiness, fear and discomfort into feelings of joy, peace and your wisdom. I ask for your strength and wisdom lord to continue your will, give me peace. Hard times, bad times, or tough times, I still have faith in you."

If you've never given up your life to care for a loved one full or part time, it's quite difficult to imagine the obstacles those who are caregivers face. Whether it's the struggle of giving up or altering finances, your time, social life, relationship status, or daily routines, the process is difficult. However, it's important that you understand there are people out there who are walking along this journey every single day. Some may seem tenser than others, yet, no matter the difficulty of the situation, we are all fully capable of coming out undefeated.

Point to ponder: The struggle is SIMPLY part of the story...

Doubting God?

"Don't lose hope. When you're down to nothing, God is up to something."

~Robert Schuler

With every assignment comes a set of instructions.

Use God and ask him for instructions on your life.

Read the instruction manual {your bible.} as often as possible.

In order to stay encouraged, follow these tips:

1. Take time to listen

2. Take time to digress

3. Practice what you've learned

4. Ask questions

Point to ponder - "With every assignment a blessing is soon to follow."

Daily dairy,

"*We must meet the challenge rather than wish it weren't before us.*"

~Unknown

Are you one to always avoid a terrible or awkward situation rather than face it? No one will notice right? Wrong? Don't allow those uncomfortable challenges to overpower you. Instead be empowered. In fact, think of all the things that scare you as of now, and cast those fears away with this prayer

"Lord, I know that I'm not perfect and I will endure several trials and tribulations, but right now I ask for Your complete authority over each and every corner of my life."

Point to ponder - When you're going through something hard and wonder where God is, remember the teacher is always silent during a test.

DAY 20

So you're not where you want to be?

"God's plans for your life exceed the circumstances of your day."

~Oprah

∞

Feeling fatigued, depressed or maybe even ill? You have come too far to give up now. First things first, take the loads of pressure off of your shoulders. Release them. Begin to take charge not only when things work in your favor, but take charge in the midst of what you're going through.

Take control today, and get back to where you want to be.

Today: Don't let your stress level dictate your day. Talk to God and make an even exchange. Give him your burdens and he'll in return provide peace.

Point to ponder: What are your goals for the days ahead?

Read 2 Corinthians 8:11

Privacy!

Once you've lost your privacy, you realize you've lost an extremely valuable thing.

~Billy Graham

∞

It's the things we take for granted that we miss the most once they're taken away. Privacy is the term, and it is also the key inner peace, sanctity and well being. Unfortunately, privacy becomes public when taking on a caring position.

The cycle will form at any point where your privacy will soon shift.

The point is, whether you're a part of the sandwich generation (caring for a loved one while also caring for your own family) or you're solely taking care of a loved one on your own, you need privacy. **We All Need Privacy!**

We all need peace, comfort and a constant reminder that whatever it is that we're going through won't last forever. So find a common ground in the household, and be cautious yet respectful of the emotions of others. It's very often in this stage that subliminal messages can be misinterpreted. Also, find a small space you can call your own in your spare time. Find it, claim it, and keep it.

Fear shall not answer upon you...

∞

What has you fearful today? Is it a new project? A difficult person? A new journey? Or in some cases fear of what tomorrow may hold? Don't be afraid.

"Peace I leave you; my peace I give you. I do not give to you as the world gives. Do not let your hearts be troubled and do not be afraid."

JOHN 12:27 (NIV)

DAY 23

Give yourself permission

∞

When I became a full time caretaker for my mother, caretaking became my #1 priority. I responded to my mother's every need, I stood by her side morning, noon and night, and even as she slept I waited there on guard for her next request. Without any doubt my mother was my main priority. I turned down relationships, date nights, outings, even personal time for myself. I very often felt guilty for even spending a couple of minutes without her.

Are you experiencing this same form of guilt? At any point in caretaking, we as Caregivers tend to confuse our duty of caring for our loved one with the understanding that we have to completely block out our own lives.

As much as your loved one may rely on your support, they still have desires for you to be happy. What's happy about delaying the life that God clearly set out for you to live in freely? Give yourself permission to live a little. Breathe a little. Smile more and do more of the things that make you happy.

Point to ponder: What is it that you want God's permission to do?

Read Acts 20:24

Life is too short

> *"Stop worrying and start praying."*
>
> ~Bill Blankschael

∞

Hearing this statement is one thing, but truly understanding God's timing for our entire life is another. Before, I would wake up every single day with no care in the world, I developed a routine, and sadly I revolved my entire life around it.

{[But things changed.]}

My mother became my patient, my grandfather passed away, several family members became ill, and sadly close friends and acquaintances passed me by.

With the mindset that I had in the beginning of this journey, I typically asked myself "Why is God testing me?" but as I opened my eyes to life itself I realized God was preparing me.

It's tough as can be at this very moment in your life. And you're not prepared. You ask God "Why now?" Why not save this test for a more suitable time in my life? Be not weary, God will never let you reach your breaking point. Remember that God has a promise over each and every one of our lives. Let him prepare you for the road ahead.

Exercise; Want to relieve that unexplainable feeling that you're experiencing? Take all of your fears, anxieties, etc. and write them down on paper.

Next, leave them right there on that very sheet of paper and in the hands of God. He will see you through.

Point to ponder: Start today with a clean slate. Leave all of your doubts, worries and mistakes in yesterday's tally, and ask God to restore the joy that comes from your salvation.

Read Psalm 51:10

No regrets

"If you feel like you can't go anymore just pray. God is listening and everything will be alright in his Perfect timing."

~Unknown

How many things over the course of your entire life could you look back on and absolutely wish they never occurred? Were they really bad? Do you wish you'd never even experienced them? Now think about your life as of now and all the accomplishments that you've made over the years. Your life may not be 100% of what you may have wanted or expected it to be. However, what if you never endured those tough times and hardships. Would you be the woman or man that you are now?

You may say to yourself that you're in the midst of a hardship now, but think of the wonderful garden God is planting.

Point to ponder: Understand that what's yours is also Gods. Your weaknesses, your failings and ultimately your victories are all there for Gods greater glory.

Read Exodus 15:13

A tragedy is a setup for triumph

"Never take your eyes off God. He never takes something away without giving back something two times Greater."

~Joyce Meyer

Ever found a time in your life where you couldn't quite explain the feelings you were experiencing? That moment was just about every single day for me. Some days I experienced the effects of stress, anxiety, depression and lack of sleep.

As if your life isn't busy enough, now you have the new responsibility of taking care of a loved one. Sure along this new journey there will be many sleepless nights, less time to do the things you enjoy, and unfortunately lots of stress.

If we knew how difficult the times ahead of us would be, would we bail or would we continue enduring them? Don't press pause on your life! Stay strong and keep pressing, you will make it.

Point to ponder: Instead of complaining, being bitter and placing yourself into an even greater predicament, begin to thank God now for the resources he's placed in front of you to work through those trials.

Read James 1:5-6

Appreciation

∞

So you woke up earlier than expected. What makes it even worse is you had a sleepless night of tossing and turning. You prepped meals, cooked, cleaned, and given all that you can possibly give, all to feel hopeless. Like the energizer bunny you have to 'keep going and going' with the thought that amongst all the things you do 7 days a week, there's very little appreciation.

The absence of appreciation from your loved one doesn't always mean that you're not doing a great job, or your work ethic has fallen, nor does it mean that you're not appreciated. Sometimes there are no words left to express ones gratitude for the many things you do.

Point to ponder: It's completely rewarding to care for a loved one; however, the experience can be quite stressful and isolating. Don't allow the enemy in on your weaknesses and don't ever feel as if you're underappreciated. Many can't stand in your shoes, <u>SO WEAR YOURS PROUDLY</u>...

What makes a caregiver happy?

"Happy is a deep sense of knowing you're in the right place at the right time, doing the right thing."

~Unknown

∞

So, what makes a caregiver happy?

1. Having friendships

2. Daily activities

3. Laughing more

4. Taking a long walk

5. Cuddling with a loved one

6. An unexpected hug from someone

7. A phone call from a loved one

8. Kindness

9. Thoughts of gratitude from others

10. Dinner and time alone

11. Privacy

12. Relaxation

13. A nice massage

14. Appreciation

15. A thank you

16. A nice surprise

17. Free time

18. Watching a nice movie

19. Reading an encouraging book

20. Sleep

Point to ponder: Evaluate some of the previous tasks and how they can be added to your schedule. Understand that the happiest people don't always have the best of everything, they tend to make the best of everything.

_P.U.S.H_

"In even the most challenging moments (Pray Until Something Happens.)"

If I were to count the number of times of has used a devastating occurrence or situation to shift me closer to him, the numbers would never add up. And in the midst of every possible thing that could go wrong in my life, it always seemed as if God wanted to punish me, when the truth is he was really drawing me closer to him.

Think about those moments when your day is less than perfect. What about those days when you've had more problems to defeat than time in a day. Think of those under the weather days.... The days when you've cared and worked so hard for others that you tend to have forgotten about yourself. Well, what about yourself? Still feel as if God is punishing you, or is it that he's pushing you into something greater?

Let's say today God wants to push you far beyond your limits. He wants to take you from the norm and release you from your comfort zone. Will you allow him to take you far beyond your limits, or will you remain where you are?

DAY 30

Express yourself

∞

During my caretaking journey, I transformed into the "yes girl." when asked if I was ok, yes was my answer, when asked if I would help out with projects my answer was yes and when asked if I had everything under control, my answer was always yes.

Now, it's safe to say that I've grown from my experiences and taken ownership of bottling my emotions. However, for others it's imperative to take ownership of your emotions and express them. Be as truthful as possible, because the truth is not for the other person it's for you.

No one knows your thoughts, feelings, and emotions to what you're dealing with but you. Don't reject yourself. You are worthy of expression, so express yourself.....You're worth it.

Tell your story

"Don't be ashamed of your story, it will inspire others."

What you are dealing with right now may have been sudden. You may have had months to prepare, or days, but what if I were to tell you that someone else would endure every single thing that has already occurred in your life?

The struggle is a part of the story, but telling your truth gives others hope for their future.

Don't be ashamed to tell others what you've endured and how difficult this journey may have been for you.

You're story gives validity to not only what God can place us through, but what he can bring you out of for his greater Glory...

THE STORY OF YOUR JOURNEY: Fill in the blank with (adj, verbs, etc.) that describe your journey.

My name is_____ and I am wonderfully made

I am _____ years young and I am a caretaker

When I began this journey I was _____

expected this process to be _____

This journey has been _____

The most important thing I've learned from this experience is

_____

I have also gained _____

To continue my journey I will

_____

To remain positive and uplifted I will

_____

"Trust in the lord with all thine heart and lean not on thine own understanding.

In all thy ways acknowledge him and he shall direct our paths."

PROVERBS 3:5-6

Today I start a challenge!

"Turn your worry list into a prayer list."

- ✓ The tame my tongue challenge...
- ✓ No boasting
- ✓ No complaining
- ✓ No anger
- ✓ No harsh words
- ✓ And accountability

In this challenge I strive hard to shift my negative thoughts and turn them into positive thoughts and feelings.

Lord, hold my tongue, open my ears, and prepare my heart for your vision. Let me be silent in times of unsureness and open to your teachings.

If we train our minds to rely strictly on thoughts of positivity we will notice changes in our inner being.

Today I start the challenge, will you?

Point to ponder: What challenge will you set for yourself today?

Read Job 33:32-33

Feeling pressure?

"God is getting ready to turn your pain into promise."

~Rick Warren

∞

Feeling useless? God doesn't. It always amazes me, how we put such harsh pressure on ourselves, only to make ourselves feel as if it's in fact God who is the one placing the pressure on us. In fact, he doesn't place pressure on us at all. He sees a valuable son, daughter, husband, wife, mother or father.

Regardless of your title, know that all that you do, whether big or small, is counted by God and we are all perfect in his eyes. Like pottery, he is molding and shaping your gift. Embrace your storm, don't be embarrassed!

Point to ponder: There is victory over fear.

Read James 1:3-13

Restless?

"God never leads us where he cannot keep us. His grace is always sufficient."

~2 Corinthians 12:9

Can't sleep at night because of the emotional build up? Has the stress increased? The pressure caused turmoil? Or does something simply weigh heavy on your heart?

Meditate on this prayer,

Lord, please give me the strength to cope. Any problem that it is that I can't solve on my own, let it be yours. May you silence my restless spirit, and give me the peace that I strongly desire.

Point to ponder: What is it that keeps you up at night? Is it work? Stress? Anxieties of what the next day may hold? Or is the cause of your restless night an empty void that only God can fill?

Read Exodus 16:8

The Daily Battle

"When you face difficult times, know that challenges are not sent to destroy you. They're sent to promote, increase and strengthen you."

~Joel Osteen

∞

Life gets harder daily, and it's a constant battle. Sometimes things may appear perfect one day, and the next day you feel as if you're on the edge.

Life is a fight, but it's also a wonderful reward. The saying that when God has something amazing in store, the enemy attempts to block your blessings is as accurate today as it was in the past... The key is, we have to stay encouraged. Read a scripture, find a quote, talk to a friend, constantly encourage yourself, so that the enemy doesn't take the time that you have alone to implant negative thoughts in your mind.

In the constant battle of life, we must trade in our fears, put on the boxing gloves, and fight off what it is that we're most afraid of. Fight for the freedom within you...

Point to ponder: Today, take a moment to retrain your thoughts. You can allow your thoughts to be used by the enemy to both hurt and hinder you, or you can allow God to work on blessing your life.

Don't condemn yourself by your thoughts and or your words, instead pray for release.

Understand that you're not the enemy.

"All things are difficult before they are easy."

~Thomas Fuller

Caring for a loved one is the least bit easy. Whether you're caring for a sick child, an elderly or ill parent, family member or friend, someone has to do the job. In the position that you're in, someone will have to make tough, yet health conscious decisions for the good of your loved one. But what you don't want to do is make the person who receives your care feel as if they're incapable of doing anything. Keep them encouraged, read with them, pray for them, and if possible allow them in on the decision making process. The inclusion of simple tasks and decisions will make the world of a difference in the way your loved one feels and it will also leave you "the giver" feeling a little less guilty.

Exhausted?

"Be not weary in well doing."

~Galatians 6:9

∞

At some point, while caring for a senior parent or loved one, most caregivers experience a feeling of emotional exhaustion or increased anxiety. These feelings are part of the signs and symptoms associated with caregiver burnout - a state of physical, emotional and mental exhaustion that's often accompanied by a change in attitude.

To help ward off these feelings, I have five tips that will help you avoid growing weary and keep caregiver burnout at bay.

1.) Talk to others about your emotions

2.) Feeling burned out can evoke feelings of fear, anger, resentment and guilt. Talk to friends or family members to help provide an outlet for negative emotions. If that's not an option, seeing a counselor or a therapist can be a good alternative.

3.) Keep up with other activities continuing to participate in activities that you enjoy is important for maintaining a sense of self through the caregiving process. Whether it's jogging, playing tennis or strolling through a museum, staying active will help stave off depression and give you boosts of much-needed energy through the day.

4.) Give yourself a break!

5.) Find time within your day to do things that you enjoy. Also, If possible, use resources available to you such as respite or home health care. Have someone (another friend or family member, or a paid caregiver) to help out a few days a week or on the weekends so that you can have time off to recharge.

6.) Educate yourself. Often, feeling prepared to handle unexpected caregiver situations can help rid those negative emotions tied to lack of caregiving knowledge.

7.) Opt for a caregiver alliance or support group

Point to ponder: There are several obstacles within a single day, which may leave one physically or mentally exhausted. But remember, "If you don't know the sweat of the work, you'll never understand the sweetness of the victory."

***Information listed according to the National Care Alliance.

LOSING A LOVED ONE

"Blessed are those who mourn for they shall be comforted."

~Matthew 5:4

∞

Grief is a natural, often intense process that, we will all at some period in our lives experience.

Losing a loved one is never easy, and the process leading up to it can often entail lots of hard work for months or sometimes years.

As profound as it sounds, the loss of a spouse, child or parent very well may affect our own Identities—considerably as a husband, wife, parent or offspring.

The arising of grief can come from a sudden change in circumstances after a death and or the fear of not knowing what lies ahead.

There are two forms of grief that we may experience. [Anticipatory and Sudden].

Anticipating what lies ahead can be just as painful as losing a life. Family members may experience guilt or shame for "wishing it were over" or seeing their loved one as already "gone" intellectually. However, It's important for one to recognize that these feelings as normal.

Grief impacts each individual differently. And it's very difficult to place a time frame on how long the period will last. The feeling may often overpower your life in the beginning, but it's imperative to allow yourself plenty of time to heal.

There are several ways of drawing strength while in bereavement, including friends, family, close acquaintances as well as professional sources.

Point to ponder: Understand that God never keeps us where he can't sustain us, therefore trust that God will supply you with all the strength, guidance, and wisdom you'll need to get by.

Read the following Scriptures:

[Romans 8:38-39] [John14:1-3] [Matthew 11:28-29]

❖ **May is National Stroke Awareness Month.**

∞

A stroke is a loss of brain function usually caused by the lack of blood connectivity to the brain.

There are two forms of stroke:

Ischemic and Hemorrhagic

Ischemic occurs when the artery that supplies the brain narrows or blocks, while a Hemorrhagic occurs when a blood vessel in the brain ruptures. (During this, blood cells lose their supply and quickly die).

According to the American Stroke Association, if one notices signs of

Face drooping- if the person notices numbness or drooping of the face. (smile)

Arm weakness-look to see if there's an unbalance in posture, dizziness or numbness. (Ask the person to

raise both arms)

Speech difficulty- the most noticeable sign will be slurred speech. An ultimate method to check, is to

Have the person repeat a simple sentence, or count 1-10.

If a person shows any of the following signs, then immediately call 911

Several factors will often increase your chances of stroke, but understanding the signs as well as adding healthier alternatives to your lifestyle will ultimately reduce your chances of being at risk.

Healthier Living

➕ Here are a few healthy benefits of some of your favorite fruits and their beneficial nutrients according to cdc.gov

Try to incorporate one or more of these into your diet for a healthier boost.

Apple	This fruit contains both flavonoids and antioxidants, which help prevent asthma and diabetes.
Tomato	This fruit contains lycopene which ultimately helps lower cholesterol and reduces an early risk of prostate cancer.

Mango	This fruit contains both Zeaxanthin and lutein, which help protect your vision.
Raspberry	This fruit contains an acid that helps prevent cancer and boost the metabolism.
Blackberry	This fruit contains anthocyanin, which are preventative of cancer and ultimately reduce the risk of stroke.
Pear	This fruit is very high in fiber, which reduces constipation, cholesterol and heart disease.
Avocado	Did you know that these fruits contain twice as much potassium as bananas? What's even better is that they also help reduce cholesterol levels.
Grape	This fruit contains resveratrol, which help lower blood pressure, the signs of blood clots and the ultimate spreading of cancer cells.
Grapefruit	This fruit contains both flavonoids and lycopene which lower cholesterol and reduce the risk of cancer.
Kiwi	Did you know that kiwi can be eaten whole*skin and all)? This fruit contains a high source of vitamin c, which helps reduce blood levels, while also protecting our bones and teeth.
Lemon	As acidic as this fruit is, it is known to prevent indigestion, fever, constipation and the lowering of blood pressure.
Cherry	This fruit contains vitamin c, which may help in reducing pain and inflammation.
Orange	This fruit is high in folate, which lowers blood pressure

Strawberry	Did you know that these sweet berries contain anti inflammatory properties? These help prevent early signs of tumors
Peach	Peaches contain vitamin a which not only helps in fighting off terrible infections, but helps build the immune system.
Blueberry	This fruit may be last on the list, but it's definitely first on the charts. Blueberries are quoted as being number one in antioxidants, which ultimately help reduce the risk of aging diseases, such as Alzheimer's and Parkinson's disease.

To care for those who once cared for us is one of the highest honors...

Robin W. Thomas
Stroke survivor/advocate
5/7/2013

WHO CARES?!

For more information on how to become involved in a caregiving group in your area, visit www.caregiver.org

For questions regarding this book, or if you'd simply like to offer feedback, please email Meagan M. Thomas at whocares.tn@gmail.com

Made in the USA
Charleston, SC
20 May 2014